TODAY'S U.S. ARMY

by DON NARDO

Major (Retired) Margaret Griffin, MS
U.S. Army
Atlanta, Georgia

COMPASS POINT BOOKS
a capstone imprint

Compass Point Books are published by Capstone,
1710 Roe Crest Drive, North Mankato, Minnesota 56003
www.capstonepub.com

Editorial Credits
Editor: Brenda Haugen
Designer: Alison Thiele
Production Specialist: Eric Manske
Library Consultant: Kathleen Baxter

Photo Credits
Corbis: Bettmann, 33; DoD photo, 21; Getty Images: Robert Nickelsberg, 24; Newscom: AFP/Luke
Frazza, 41, EPA/Erik S. Lesser, 35, European Press Agency/Sergei_Chirikov, 5, ZUMA Press, 15,
23, ZUMA Press/SNAP, 39 (top); Photo by 1st Lt. Barry Eason, National Guard Marksmanship
Training Center, 28; U.S. Air Force photo by Master Sgt. Mike Buytas, 27, Master Sgt. Toby M.
Valadie, 9, Senior Airman Micky M. Bazaldua, 17, Senior Airman Tony R. Ritter, 37, Tech. Sgt.
Bradley C. Church, 32, Tech. Sgt. Chris Hibben, 13, Tech Sgt. Michele A. Desrochers, 29; U.S. Army
photo, 25, 30, D. Myles Cullen, 19, Michael J. MacLeod, 43, Pfc. F.C. Phillips, 38, Sgt. John Crosby,
cover (top), Spc. Sherrod Percell, 6, Staff Sgt. Tracy Hohman, 31, T4c. Messerlin, 39 (bottom),
Tommy Gilligan/West Point Public Affairs, 22; U.S. Navy photo by MC2 Eli J. Medellin, cover
(bottom), 1, MC3 Joshua Nistas, 12

Artistic Effects
Shutterstock: doodle, Ewa Walicka, Kilmukhametov Art, W.J.

Library of Congress Cataloging-in-Publication Data
Nardo, Don, 1947-
  Today's U.S. Army/by Don Nardo; consultant, Margaret Griffin.
    p. cm. — (The U.S. Armed Forces)
  Includes bibliographical references.
  Audience: Grades 4-6.
  ISBN 978-0-7565-4618-2 (library binding)
  ISBN 978-0-7565-4635-9 (paperback)
  ISBN 978-0-7565-4673-1 (ebook PDF)
1. Griffin, Margaret, MS. 2. United States. Army—Juvenile literature. I. Title.
  UA25.N364 2014
  355.00973—dc23   2012009990

Printed in the United States of America in Brainerd, Minnesota.
092012   006938BANGS13

TABLE OF CONTENTS

CHAPTER ONE:

FIGHTING TERROR

On October 7, 2001, just 26 days after the worst terrorist attack on United States soil, the U.S. Army and other forces invaded Afghanistan. The goal of the invasion, called Operation Enduring Freedom, was to destroy the terrorist group al-Qaeda and topple the Taliban, which protected it. Afghanistan was known as a training ground and safe haven for terrorists, including many of those responsible for the September 11, 2001, attacks on the United States that killed nearly 3,000 people.

With little time to prepare, Army Special Forces teams landed deep in hostile territory in Afghanistan. Timing was critical. The mountainous Asian nation's harsh winters are legendary. Military officials wanted to capture a strategic Afghan city before winter set in.

The fighting was fierce, but it didn't take long for the Army and its allies, dubbed the Northern Alliance, to reach their goal. On November 13, the Afghan capital of Kabul fell to Northern Alliance forces, which included about 1,300 U.S. troops. Most members of al-Qaeda fled. But Operation Enduring Freedom continued. The Army would not give up on its mission to root out terrorists, especially those responsible for the September 11 tragedy.

U.S forces dropped bombs on Taliban positions in northeastern Afghanistan in November 2001.

THE ARMY'S PURPOSE

Enduring Freedom showed the U.S. Army at its best. The Army is one of the five branches of America's military. The main purpose of all five—the Army, Navy, Marines, Air Force, and Coast Guard—is to defend the United States.

U.S. soldiers trained for a mission during Operation Enduring Freedom.

In the period following the 9/11 attacks, the enemy was based on land. U.S. Army soldiers are mainly land fighters. So they were the primary responders during the crisis. In fact, the Army often takes the lead in the land portions of the nation's military conflicts.

Of course, if there were no attacks or wars, no armies would be needed. But wars do occur. Military historian John C. McManus explains that "humanity has a fatal flaw." It is a tendency "to make war." He adds, "Wars have marred the entire span of human history. They continue to do so today. There is no reason to believe that the future will be any different." That is why the U.S. Army is necessary.

The Army's size has varied over the years. It comes as no surprise that it was the biggest during major wars. During World War II (1939-1945), for example, it had more than 8 million members.

In recent times the U.S. Army has been much smaller. In 2012 it had 560,000 active soldiers. About 86 percent were men.

The Army also had 645,000 backup soldiers in 2012. Some belonged to the U.S. Army Reserve. Others were members of the Army National Guard. These soldiers usually serve one weekend a month. In an emergency they can be called to active duty.

THE ARMY'S ORIGINS

In April 1775 British soldiers battled with American colonists. Several men died on both sides. In response, rebel colonial leaders created their own military force. They called it the Continental Army. George Washington was its first commander. Over time, it became known as the U.S. Army.

ARMY CULTURE

Those Americans who join the Army soon get used to its culture—its way of life.

For instance, most people working on an Army installation or facility rise very early in the morning. They also have their own way of telling time, using a 24-hour clock that begins at midnight. Noon is "twelve hundred," written as "1200." Five o'clock is "1700." Also, the soldiers wear uniforms when on duty. They must be well groomed at all times. In addition, they are required to salute officers of higher ranks. It is also customary to call an officer "sir" or "ma'am."

THE MILITARY ALPHABET

Among the many aspects of Army culture is the military alphabet. It includes all the letters in the regular English alphabet. But in this case, each letter has a word to express it. This is done to make sure vital parts of spoken messages are clear and free of mistakes. For example, the word cat would be expressed as "Charlie, Alpha, Tango." Some of these military words are listed:

A .... Alpha

B .... Bravo

C............ Charlie

D .... Delta

F............ Foxtrot

K .... Kilo

O .... Oscar

T............ Tango

V .... Victor

Z............ Zulu

Another part of Army culture is concerned with values. Leaders try to instill a sense of duty. They also emphasize teamwork. These make a unit of soldiers, and the Army in general, work better to achieve a shared goal. Almost always that goal is the mission at hand.

Saluting a higher ranking officer is a sign of respect.

9

CHAPTER TWO:
ARMY ORGANIZATION AND JOBS

In order to succeed and complete its missions, any military force must be efficient. The U.S. Army is highly efficient. In part, this is because it is well organized.

The Army has an ordered chain of command. It is designed to pass orders from someone in authority to those who will carry out those orders. The United States is a democracy. So its highest military leaders are civilians. This helps to keep the military from wielding too much power in the country. The head of all the military branches, including the Army, is the president. Next in line is another civilian, the secretary of defense.

Beneath the secretary of defense are the top two Army leaders. One is the secretary of the Army. He or she is a civilian. The other, who holds equal rank, is the Army chief of staff. The Army chief of staff is the highest-ranking military officer in the Army. One of this person's main jobs is to act as military adviser to the secretary of the Army.

Next in the chain of command are the other Army officers. The highest ranked are the generals. Beneath them are those holding the rank of colonel, then lieutenant colonel. Then come the ranks of major, captain, first lieutenant, and second lieutenant.

Ranked beneath the officers are the enlisted soldiers. Top ranked among them are the sergeants. Then come the corporals. Lowest in the chain are the privates. Nearly all Army soldiers wear insignia on their uniforms. The insignia indicate their individual ranks, their branch in the Army, and their unit.

ARMY JOBS

The U.S. Army has a very well organized structure. It is broken down into units of various sizes, from small squads to huge field armies. Within the Army's unit, soldiers perform a wide range of jobs. "The number of careers and jobs that are available to individuals serving in the Army is virtually unlimited," said an active duty soldier.

One of these jobs lies at the Army's core. It involves groups of fighters called infantry. Their task is to engage an enemy directly in battle. The infantry is vital to the Army's success. But those fighters could not operate without the aid of many others. Some soldiers transport and repair heavy equipment, for instance. This includes tanks, trucks, cannons, and rockets.

ARMY STRUCTURE • • • • • • • • • • •

Unit	Size	Leader
Squad	4 to 10 soldiers	Sergeant or staff sergeant
Platoon	2 to 4 squads	Lieutenant
Company	3 to 5 platoons	Captain
Battalion	3 to 6 companies	Lieutenant colonel
Brigade	3 or more battalions	Colonel or brigadier general
Division	3 brigades	General
Corps	2 to 5 divisions	General
Field army	2 to 5 corps	General

Meanwhile, engineers build or repair roads and bridges used by the infantry and other ground-based units. Members of the Army's food service make sure that everyone is fed. There are also medics who take care of injured soldiers during battle. Surgeons perform operations in Army hospitals. Other Army health-care jobs are filled by doctors, nurses, dentists, and lab workers.

There are also communications experts. They send and receive radio signals. Such signals can contain orders or important news. Other soldiers are involved in supply services. Their job is to ensure that fighters have uniforms, packs, and weapons. They also store and distribute spare parts for trucks and other heavy equipment.

Army mechanics work on a vehicle's engine.

A meal is served during a training exercise at Fort Hunter Liggett in California.

THE ARMY'S ENGINEERS

The Army even has its own police officers. Military police, called MPs, enforce Army rules. They also protect Army posts and guard prisoners. In addition, some MPs try to solve crimes, as civilian detectives do. In fact, the Army has a large proportion of the same jobs that exist outside the military.

The Army Corps of Engineers dates back to 1779. At the time it consisted of one engineer and two assistants. Today the corps has more than 37,000 military and civilian members. Their job is to design and build canals, dams, and bridges. They also erect levees, power plants, and other large-scale structures.

CHAPTER THREE:

ENLISTING IN THE ARMY

Every year thousands of young men and women enlist in the U.S. Army. Their reasons for joining vary widely. Some join because of strong feelings of love for their country. Others feel that Army life will teach them to be more disciplined. Still others are looking for job training or other sorts of education. Some make a career out of the Army.

Those with such motives almost always find the Army rewarding. Army life features strict rules. So all who join learn better discipline. Also, all soldiers receive extensive job training. Other benefits include excellent medical and dental care. The Army provides 30 days of paid vacation called leave each year. In addition, when a soldier's service is done, he or she can use the GI Bill. It helps military veterans pay for college.

Someone who decides to join the Army must go through the standard enlistment process. It involves a wide range of questions and tests. They are designed to find out if a person is qualified and fit to join.

To join the U.S. Army, a person must be from 18 to 42 years old. A person who is 17 years old can join if he or she has parental consent. A recruit must also be a U.S. citizen, though some citizens of other nations who live legally in the United States can join. Recruits also must have a high school diploma or GED (general education development) certificate.

New Army recruits arrive at a training station in Fort Knox, Kentucky.

Applicants need to be physically fit as well. In part, this refers to being in good condition. More important is for a person to be free of certain serious ailments. Cancer and heart disease are examples. So are a badly curved spine and blindness in one eye.

Also, a person who desires to enlist in the Army must not be using illegal drugs. All applicants receive drug and alcohol tests. Anyone who fails is not allowed to join. Soldiers must remain drug free, although the Army offers treatment to those who slip. All soldiers are retested for drugs from time to time. This is done partly to make certain they remain healthy. But it also ensures that no one will endanger other soldiers or cause a mission to fail. Military officer Scott A. Ostrow points out, "Would you want to fly in an airplane if there was a chance that the pilot or mechanic who works on the plane used drugs?"

BACKGROUND CHECKS

Every applicant to the U.S. Army goes through a background check. It is to make sure the person has not committed any crimes. Army investigators look into the applicant's past. They contact all schools the person attended. They also ask the police if the applicant has a criminal record. In addition, all people applying for the Army are fingerprinted.

Recruits wait in a lab for their blood tests during training.

PASSING THE TEST

All applicants to the Army take the ASVAB—the Armed Services Vocational Aptitude Battery. The exam measures a person's skills and knowledge.

Lasting up to three hours, it consists of multiple-choice questions. They test the applicant's abilities in reading, math, science, and other areas. They also show if he or she has mechanical skills.

Someone who scores very low on the test is not allowed to join the Army. However, very few applicants score that low. For the most part, the ASVAB is designed to show where a person's talents lie. The test can show the jobs he or she would likely do best. For example, someone who scores high in the mechanical portions of the test would likely be assigned to work with mechanical devices.

An applicant who has met all the requirements is ready to formally enlist. The process consists of taking an oath. It is a serious ceremony that no one

takes lightly. After all, the person's life is about to change in major ways. To reflect the importance of the oath, it is conducted by an Army officer. The officer faces the enlistee, who raises the right hand and states:

Army recruits in New York City take the oath of enlistment.

"I do solemnly swear that I will support and defend the Constitution of the United States against all enemies, foreign and domestic; that I will bear true faith and allegiance to the same; and that I will obey the orders of the President of the United States and the orders of the officers appointed over me, according to regulations and the Uniform Code of Military Justice. So help me God."

19

CHAPTER FOUR:
TRAINING TO BECOME A SOLDIER

After someone has enlisted in the Army, he or she must go through basic training. Training for the new recruits lasts 10 weeks. It takes place at one of several posts around the United States. Male and female recruits train together, except for combat preparation. To date, women are still not officially assigned to combat. But they often find themselves in combat situations and have no choice but to fight.

WOMEN IN THE ARMY

Today both men and women enlist in the Army and receive training. But this was not always the case. When the Army first formed in the late 1700s, women could not join. Still, a number of women did serve in every U.S. war. At first they did it by dressing like and pretending to be men. Eventually they were allowed to serve as Army nurses and office workers.

More than 12,000 women filled such positions in World War I (1914–1918). That number rose to more than 400,000 in World War II. In 1942 Congress established the WAACs, the Women's Army Auxiliary Corps. The group's name eventually was shortened to Women's Army Corps. Over time, members of the WACs came to fill the same kinds

Private Martha D. Young served as an aircraft mechanic during World War II.

of noncombat Army jobs done by men. Some women became officers as well. The WACs were eliminated in 1978. Since then women have been regular members of the Army along with men. The rules still forbid women from being purposely assigned to combat. But in reality, many women are engaged in combat, and there are many calls to eliminate the ban. The Pentagon is considering opening up more jobs to women.

THE BEST POSSIBLE SHAPE

The first week of training is devoted to orientation. A sergeant shows the recruits around the post and tells them about military life. They learn where to sleep and eat. They also find out where to go for medical treatment if needed. Recruits receive ID cards and uniforms. In addition, the male recruits get their first military haircuts, which are very short. Perhaps the most important things to learn are the rules of conduct. They include saluting officers and following orders to the letter.

In the second week on the post, recruits begin their physical training. They are divided into platoons. Each platoon has about 20 to 40 members. The chief trainer is called a drill sergeant. He or she is usually a tough, no-nonsense person. The sergeant works the recruits hard because they must get into the best possible shape. The Army's physical fitness manual states it well: "The objective of physical training in the Army is to enhance the soldiers' abilities to meet the physical demands of war." So it is not surprising that the recruits perform many difficult exercises. They also endure grueling obstacle courses. They include climbing walls and ropes and crawling on their

Each male recruit is required to have a very short military haircut.

Recruits train on an obstacle course under the direction of a drill instructor.

bellies. Recruits must also run up to 2 miles (3.2 kilometers) each day. They also learn to fight hand-to-hand. Finally, they master the use of combat rifles and other handheld weapons.

The recruits live in dormlike structures called barracks. Some barracks are for men, and others are for women. Many barracks have one large room containing beds and lockers. A recruit keeps personal belongings in a locker. Each barrack is equipped with a large communal bathroom. The recruits are expected to keep the showers, sinks, and toilets clean at all times.

In a typical day, the recruits wake up at 4:30 a.m. They exercise and then march to the mess hall, a building where meals are served. They have 10 minutes to eat breakfast, after which they return to the barracks, shower, get dressed, and make their beds. Then their day of regular training begins.

TAKING THE OFFICER ROUTE

After finishing basic training, the recruits are full-fledged soldiers. Their initial rank is private. Over time some may be promoted to corporal or sergeant.

In contrast, someone who wants a career as an Army officer must train specially for it. One way to do so is to attend the United States Military Academy. It is located at

West Point, New York. Founded in 1802, West Point was the nation's first military service college. To get in, one has to be nominated. The nomination must come from the Department of the Army, another branch of the service, or a member of Congress.

At first West Point accepted only men. In 1976, however, it opened its doors to women. Today about 4,400 men and women attend the school each year.

West Point freshmen go through basic training.

OTHER WAYS TO BECOME AN OFFICER

West Point cadets celebrate their graduation by tossing their hats.

Those who want to be Army officers do not have to attend West Point. They can also go to Officer Candidate School, in Fort Benning, Georgia. A person must have some college experience to get in. He or she also has to be in the Army already. Still another way to become an officer is by participating in ROTC, the Reserve Officers' Training Corps, a program offered by many universities. Students take military courses along with their regular college studies. When one graduates, he or she is an officer in the Army reserve.

The students, called cadets, go through some of the same basic training that regular recruits do. In addition, the cadets follow up with a wide range of courses. They include history, political science, and math. The cadets also study foreign languages. If a cadet's grades are good, after four years he or she graduates and attains the rank of second lieutenant.

25

CHAPTER FIVE:
SOLDIERS' GEAR AND WEAPONS

The U.S. Army supplies its soldiers with more than just excellent training. Army gear and weapons are equally top-notch. The gear consists of the special clothes and equipment the soldiers use. Their weapons are of two types. One is small arms—those they carry themselves. The other group features larger-scale devices, such as tanks and helicopters equipped with weapons.

The uniforms soldiers wear for combat are called battle dress. Patterns and colors vary according to where the soldiers are fighting. The object is to help the soldiers blend in as much as possible with the natural surroundings. In desert settings the uniforms are tan with brown spots. In forested regions soldiers wear camouflage. It features uneven splotches of green, tan, and brown.

Body armor is another common kind of gear. Worn like a vest, it is made of Kevlar. The extremely tough material resists bullets from some small arms. The soldiers' helmets are made from a very hard and tough form of plastic. The helmets are lightweight but several times stronger than steel. They can stop bullets from handguns and many rifles. Helmets worn by Army commandos are rigged with earphones. They allow a fighter to communicate with other members of his unit.

Army soldiers performed security duties during a 2006 mission in Iraq.

A soldier also carries a backpack commonly called a rucksack. Inside are food, water, and a first-aid kit. There is also a gas mask that allows the person to breathe in smoky, dusty, or poisonous air. Another useful piece of gear is a set of night vision goggles, which allow a soldier to see in the dark.

RIFLES AND GRENADES

The Army issues its fighters a highly effective rifle—the M4. It is a somewhat shorter version of the M16A2, which was standard for several years.

The two weapons are similar in many ways. But the M4 is more successful for combat in close quarters. That makes it ideal for urban fighting. The M4 weighs

An Army sniper is armed with an M24 rifle.

A soldier uses a grenade launcher mounted on his M4 rifle.

only around 7 pounds (3 kilograms). So it is easy to carry and use. Because it shoots between 700 and 950 rounds per minute, it is very deadly. The Army expects to begin upgrading to an even better version of the weapon in the next few years.

The Army's best marksmen use another weapon—the M24 sniper rifle. With it, a shooter can hit a small target at a distance of three-quarters of a mile (1.2 km).

All soldiers learn to use grenades. They are like small bombs that spray tiny pieces of metal in all directions when they explode. Some can be mounted onto and fired from an M4.

29

ARMORED VEHICLES

Among the Army's most valuable larger-scale weapons are its armored vehicles. The heaviest is the M1A2 Abrams tank. It carries a crew of four. A military researcher calls it "a brilliant platform from which to fight wars." This is partly because the M1A2 is well protected by thick armor. Also, it fires a powerful cannon that smashes enemy buildings and vehicles to bits.

A smaller tank used by the Army is the M3 Bradley fighting vehicle. It carries a crew of three. One of its main jobs is to carry fighters safely across a battlefield.

More flexible as an armored vehicle is the Stryker. Instead of treads, like other tanks, it has wheels. There are eight wheels in all. They give it more mobility and speed. Larger tanks can move little more

Stryker armored vehicles

30

An Apache helicopter takes off from a base in Afghanistan.

than 40 miles (64 km) per hour. But the Stryker can travel faster than 60 mph (97 kph). In addition, the Stryker features quite a bit of firepower. It has a small cannon and a large machine gun. It can also launch a grenade every six seconds.

The U.S. Army wields awesome firepower from the air as well. Chief among its flying armored machines is the AH-64D Apache helicopter. It is equipped with a machine gun. The Apache also carries several small but lethal missiles. One observer writes: "The Apache helicopter is the most marvelous flying machine to have graced the skies. It was . . . the first [helicopter] to pack so much fire power that it [is] often called the flying tank.

[Overall, it is] a flying machine capable of immense destruction."

Coupled with its well-trained soldiers, the military weapons are awe-inspiring. They make the U.S. Army the best and most feared army in the world.

THE AWESOME APACHE

The Apache helicopter excels because it has many advanced features. Two powerful engines can each support the helicopter by itself. So if one engine is destroyed, there is a backup. Also, strong armor that stops most kinds of bullets protects the Apache. In addition, the awesome helicopter can operate in sandstorms and other harsh conditions.

CHAPTER SIX:
ARMY SPECIAL OPERATIONS

Besides its regular soldiers, the U.S. Army has several groups of elite troops. They belong to the Special Operations Command. That wing of the Army is centered at Fort Bragg, North Carolina. Special Operations is sometimes called special ops. Its three best-known units are the Army Rangers, the Special Forces (Green Berets), and Delta Force. The units have one major task—to carry out missions that are too difficult for ordinary soldiers. A former member of the military describes one kind of mission all special ops units are good at. It is "to sneak up on the enemy and kill them without dying themselves."

The Rangers are special combat foot soldiers. They are classified as "light" infantry because they don't travel with tanks and other heavy equipment. The Rangers perform dangerous, risky missions. For example, they parachute into the midst of battles. They also capture enemy airfields and ambush enemy bases. In addition, all Rangers are skilled teachers. They often show others how to fight and survive in wartime.

A Special Forces soldier uses a rope to climb out of a helicopter during training.

ROGERS' RANGERS •

Members of the Special Operations Command serve with the memory of those who have gone before them. Among those who came before were Rogers' Rangers (above). The elite group of soldiers was created by Major Robert Rogers. He was a soldier in Britain's American colonies. In 1756 he recruited and trained fellow colonists to help the British fight the French in the French and Indian War. The Rangers carried out a series of raids against the French and their Indian allies. The missions required crossing enemy territory quickly and in secret. In later years Rogers' Rangers became a model for elite Army fighters.

Rangers go through extremely hard training that lasts 56 days. Recruits train up to 19 hours a day, seven days a week. They greatly enhance their physical conditioning. They also become experts at surviving in the wilderness. With little or no food or sleep, they climb mountains and cross rivers. Rangers also learn how to survive in junglelike conditions. The Rangers master numerous firearms during their training. They also become experts in explosives.

The Army's Special Forces, known as the Green Berets after the caps they wear, formed in 1952. The group's members perform most of the same missions the Rangers do. But the Special Forces also carry out anti-terrorist actions. The Green Berets complete political missions too. For instance, they meet and mingle with people who are hostile to the United States. Winning the hearts and minds of such potential enemies can make them allies.

ORIGINS OF THE GREEN BERET

The beret worn by members of the Army Special Forces dates back to World War II. Elite British commandos sometimes wore such caps. During the war a few American soldiers served with the commandos. Those Americans later received green berets to celebrate their service. In 1961 President John F. Kennedy and the Department of the Army gave the OK for the U.S. Special Forces to officially wear the green beret.

Rangers dive from a Blackhawk helicopter during a demonstration for military leaders.

The Special Forces go through the same basic training as the Rangers. But the Special Forces train even longer—up to a year or more.

Members are very proud of their history and deeds. Part of that pride is in their personal commitment and honor. They memorize and live by a strict honor code. Called the Special Forces Creed, it says in part:

"I will do all that my nation requires of me. … I pledge to uphold the honor and integrity of their legacy in all that I am—in all that I do. I will keep my mind and body clean, alert and strong … for this is my debt to those who depend on me."

The only thing well known about Delta Force, another celebrated Army special ops unit, is its name. Almost everything about it is top secret. What seems certain, though, is that it's the Army's most elite force. Members go through the hardest training and perform the most dangerous missions. In particular, they try to rescue hostages in seemingly impossible

circumstances. Their missions have often succeeded. Without doubt, all Americans owe them and other special ops soldiers a huge debt.

Special Operations soldiers load Zodiac boats onto a Chinook helicopter.

CHAPTER SEVEN:
THE U.S. ARMY IN ACTION

Members of the U.S. Army have fought in all of America's wars. Millions of men and women served with bravery and honor. Many even died for their country. Only their family, friends, and fellow soldiers know the exploits of most of them.

But a few ordinary soldiers did become national heroes. One was Alvin C. York (1887–1964). During World War I, he attacked German machine gun nests. York killed more than 25 enemy soldiers and captured another 132. For these feats York received the Medal of Honor. He also achieved lasting fame

thanks to a movie about him. Released in 1941, it was titled *Sergeant York*. Popular film star Gary Cooper played York.

Alvin C. York

off close to 200 others. In 1955 Murphy played himself in a film about his exploits. It was titled *To Hell and Back*.

A number of Army generals also became famous. A few even went on to become major political figures. Dwight D. Eisenhower (1890–1969) is a good example. In World War II he led the Americans and their allies in Europe. Later he was elected president of the United States. He served two terms, from 1953 to 1961.

Audie Murphy (1924–1971) was another American soldier honored in a movie. He is often called the Army's most decorated soldier. He won dozens of awards for his outstanding service in World War II. Among them is the highly prized Medal of Honor. He also received two Silver Stars, two Bronze Stars, and three Purple Hearts. In World War II he held off six enemy tanks. He also killed at least 50 German soldiers and single-handedly held

Dwight D. Eisenhower

39

FIREBALLS IN THE DESERT

The world wars were not the only ones in which U.S. soldiers performed admirably. Each of America's wars produced its share of heroes. During these conflicts the Army saw both large- and small-scale action. World War II had the highest number of big battles. But a few prominent examples have occurred since then.

GREAT, BUT NOT PERFECT

One of the greatest but also most controversial U.S. Army generals was Douglas MacArthur (1880–1964). He graduated from West Point in 1903 and served in World War I. But his most famous exploits took place in World War II and the Korean War. Some of his actions in those conflicts were brilliant. But he also made some major mistakes. Although he was a talented leader, he could also be proud and stubborn.

Notable was one that took place during the 1991 Persian Gulf War. Iraqi leader Saddam Hussein had seized the neighboring country of Kuwait. With its allies, the United States set out to free Kuwait. On February 26, 1991, Saddam's and the U.S. Army's tank forces clashed in the Iraqi desert. Some experts have called it the last great tank battle of the 20th century.

Many involved in the action said it was like hell on Earth. The American tanks outdid the Iraqi ones. One U.S. soldier later said that the enemy tanks "erupted into" countless "fireballs." These explosions "hurled debris 100 feet into the air." Smaller blasts "destroyed the vehicles beyond recognition." The American victory was complete. U.S. Army forces demolished more than 160 enemy tanks.

ACHIEVER OF MANY FIRSTS • • • • • • • • • • • • •

Colin Powell (born 1937) was among the more gifted members of the U.S. Army. He started out as a lieutenant after completing officer training. Then he fought in the Vietnam War (1959–1975). During that conflict he was wounded and received a Purple Heart. Powell also collected the Bronze Star for bravery. After the war he steadily rose through the Army's ranks. In 1989 he was promoted to four-star general. That same year he was appointed chairman of the Joint Chiefs of Staff. He was the youngest person ever to reach that high position. He was also the first African-American to serve as a Joint Chief. Another major first for Powell occurred in 2001 when he became the first African-American to serve as U.S. secretary of state (above).

SECURING THE BRIDGE

America's wars have also featured many small, little-known battles. U.S. Army special ops units fought in a number of them. Some of these units saw action in Panama in 1989, for example. The U.S. military went there to remove the brutal dictator Manuel Noriega. An important early objective was to secure a bridge over the Pacora River. Members of a special ops team approached the structure. Enemy troop carriers were already starting to cross. A military observer says it became a race "to see who would take the bridge first." The commandos "opened up on" the enemy forces with automatic weapons fire. Then the special ops fighters started firing grenades at their opponents.

The American commandos managed to secure the bridge. It was only one of numerous successful U.S. Army actions over the years. The Army's soldiers take pride in their achievements. So do the American people. All are confident these soldiers will continue to do their duty. Along with the other military branches, the Army will go on protecting the country and its interests.

A U.S. soldier provided security after a 2012 firefight in Afghanistan.

GLOSSARY

barracks—the dormlike buildings in which soldiers sleep on a military base

beret—a small cloth cap

Bronze Star—a medal given to members of the U.S. military for acts of courage and merit

cadet—a military officer in training

camouflage—patterns and colors designed to make military uniforms, gear, and weapons blend in with a given natural setting

chain of command—the ladder of Army ranks, with private at the bottom and general at the top; civilian leaders are also part of the chain of command

civilian—a person who is not in the armed forces

commando—an elite, specially trained soldier who is assigned to difficult, dangerous missions

corps—an Army unit containing 20,000 to 40,000 soldiers

culture—a set of customs, laws, and ways of speaking and acting that are followed by a group's members

enlisted soldiers—soldiers who join the Army and after basic training make up the organization's junior ranks

field army—an Army unit made up of two to five corps

GI bill—legislation providing financial aid to military veterans for attending college and buying homes; GI is slang for an enlisted soldier

infantry—foot soldiers; light infantry are soldiers who travel without tanks and other heavy weapons

insignia—badges, emblems, logos, and other symbols denoting military ranks and units

Medal of Honor—the United States' highest award for bravery in combat

medic—a military medical technician similar to an EMT

MP—short for military police, a soldier who enforces military rules

Purple Heart—a medal given to members of the U.S. military who have been wounded in action

recruit—an enlisted soldier in basic training

round—a bullet or other projectile fired by a gun

special ops—short for Special Operations Forces, consisting of the Army's elite units of soldiers

SOURCE NOTES

Chapter 1: Fighting Terror
Page 7, line 12: John C. McManus. *Grunts: Inside the American Infantry Combat Experience, World War II Through Iraq.* New York: NAL Caliber, 2010, p. 8.

Chapter 2: Army Organization and Jobs
Page 11, line 7: "Basic Army Opportunities." 24 Oct. 2012. www.usarmy.com/basic_army_opportunities/

Chapter 3: Enlisting in the Army
Page 16, col. 2, line 10: Scott A. Ostrow. *A Guide to Joining the Military.* Lawrenceville, N.J.: Thomson/Arco, 2004, p. 23.
Page 19, line 1: Ibid, p. 86.

Chapter 4: Training to Become a Soldier
Page 22, col. 2, line 12: Department of the Army. *U.S. Army Physical Fitness Guide.* Long Island City, N.Y.: Hatherleigh Press, 2002, p. 1-15.

Chapter 5: Soldiers' Gear and Weapons
Page 30, line 6: Samuel A. Southworth *U.S. Armed Forces Arsenal.* Cambridge, Mass.: Da Capo, 2004, p. 107.
Page 31, line 14: Mert Ozge, "Apache Helicopter." 24 Oct. 2012. http://ezinearticles.com/?Apache-Helicopter&id=5856340

Chapter 6: Army Special Operations
Page 32, line 14: Rod Powers, "U.S. Military Special Operations Forces." 24 Oct. 2012. http://usmilitary.about.com/od/jointservices/a/specialops.htm
Page 36, line 11: "Special Forces Creed." 24 Oct. 2012. http://sfalx.com/h_sf_creed.htm

Chapter 7: The U.S. Army in Action
Page 40, col. 2, line 16: *Grunts: Inside the American Infantry Combat Experience, World War II Through Iraq*, p. 316.
Page 42, line 11: "Operation Just Cause." 24 Oct. 2012. www.specialoperations.com/Operations/Just_Cause/Operation_Profile4.htm

READ MORE

Adams, Simon. *Soldier*. London: DK Publishing, 2009.

Dolan, Edward F. *Careers in the U.S. Army*.
New York: Marshall Cavendish, 2010.

Holmes, Richard. *Battle*. London: DK Publishing, 2009.

Llanas, Sheila Griffin. *Women of the U.S. Army*.
Mankato, Minn.: Capstone Press, 2011.

Sandler, Michael. *Army Rangers in Action*. New York: Bearport, 2008.

Simons, Lisa M. Bolt. *Soldiers of the U.S. Army*.
Mankato, Minn.: Capstone Press, 2009.

INTERNET SITES

Use FactHound to find Internet sites related to this book. All of the sites on FactHound have been researched by our staff.

Here's all you do:

Visit *www.facthound.com*

Type in this code: 9780756546182

Army Enlist
www.armyenlist.com
A site designed to start the Army enlistment process

GoArmy.com
www.goarmy.com
A site designed to provide general information about the Army and help potential enlistees make up their minds

The United States Army
www.army.mil/join
The official website of the U.S. Army contains links to extensive information about the Army, National Guard, and Army Reserve

TITLES IN THIS SERIES:

TODAY'S U.S. **AIR FORCE**

TODAY'S U.S. **ARMY**

TODAY'S U.S. **MARINES**

TODAY'S U.S. **NATIONAL GUARD**

TODAY'S U.S. **NAVY**

INDEX

ABOUT THE AUTHOR

Award-winning historian and writer Don Nardo has published many books for young people. A number of them cover various aspects of military history, including overviews of many of America's wars and studies of warfare and military weapons in ancient, medieval, and modern times. Nardo lives with his wife, Christine, in Massachusetts.